PRAISE FOR *THE THIRD BEAT*

AF279305

"Lavín's essays are an intoxicating brew of honesty and heart. This is a collection to read when you're lost and return to after you find your way. Sharp and furious, gentle and understanding, the way Lavín writes life will make you forget to breathe. *The Third Beat* seduced me from page one."
—LJ Pemberton, author of *Still Alive*

"Lauren Lavín's debut essay collection is a phenomenal work of full-bodied honesty. *The Third Beat* is a book for anyone who's found it hard to see or be themselves in a world that demands we carry the weight of its constant and, often erroneous, perceptions, i.e. everyone. The best non-fiction I've read this year."
—Jillian Luft, author of *Scumbag Summer*

"Lauren Lavín's *The Third Beat* is a visceral, spellbinding meditation on the body, both how to inhabit it more fully and how to leave it, and how sometimes that looks like the same thing. Lavín's work rides that thrilling edge between excruciation and euphoria, digging into the uncomfortable gray, and the effect is a raw, bloody honesty which blurs and deepens everything surrounding it. You cannot be fully open to the beauty of life without being intimate with death, and Lavín knows that. Meaning: you want to feel fucking alive? Read this book."
—Emily Costa, author of *Girl on Girl*

"In under a hundred pages, Lauren Lavín's essays in *The Third Beat* boldly cover sex, art, comedy, the body, travel, and, of course, death. She writes with blunt ferocity, unapologetic about the desire to be seen and wanted. I'd follow her voice anywhere she leads me. Maybe right off a cliff."
—Kristen Felicetti, author of *Log Off*

"I love seeing the world through Lauren Lavín's eyes. *The Third Beat* has the same effortlessly cool depiction of adolescence on the fringes as cult classics like *Reality Bites* and *Slacker.* Full of Bay Area punk shows, skater boys, and garage bands, Lavín's essay collection is a portal to another time—but instead of the soft-edged nostalgia these types of stories are so often packaged in, her prose reveals the pain of yearning to belong in a world not built for outcasts. Like the people in these stories, *The Third Beat* is as cool as it is honest."
—Shelby Hinte, author of *Howling Women*

"*The Third Beat* reimagines the essay collection as an altar—a lyric meditation on ghosts, night terrors, and self-destruction. It chronicles an era defined by skate parks, indie bands, and pre-internet ventures where a slimy entrepreneur could build a billion dollar business in a trash can. Lavín writes the way Frida Kahlo paints: visceral self-revelations, brutal in their honesty, that will leave readers devastated, alive, and begging for more."
—Ryan-Ashley Anderson, Managing Editor of *Pool Party*, and Kevin Maloney, author of *The Red-Headed Pilgrim*

The Third Beat

Lauren Lavín

Autofocus Books
Easton, Pennsylvania

©Lauren Lavín, 2026
All rights reserved.

Published by Autofocus Books
autofocusbooks.com

Essays/Literature
ISBN: 978-1-957392-46-2
Library of Congress Control Number: 2025949100

Cover design by Amy Wheaton

The Third Beat

First, A Small Prayer to Santa Muerte

The first time I read your name, tears poured out of me without urging and without sadness.

Table of Contents

Correcaminos

Screaming desert air shoves the car so I can't think of any music to listen to with Michael. He's grouchy, been drunk since before we flew out of Seattle this morning ("I have a drug addiction," he says easily, in warm amber tones). It's dark. People are speeding. I'm speeding. He's older than me, has lived harder, and just learned he has an autoimmune disease. He's terrified to die.

From under the corner of our sleazy motel room door, an urgent stream of water trickles to the concrete. Michael's eyes get bigger and sparklier. He slips the key card into the slot and opens the door, which sloshes through the inch or more of water inside and creates a shallow wave that pours over the doorstep and our sneakers.

Michael gets the hotel manager, who is unsurprised by the flood. I'm getting used to the way Michael befriends every person he sees. He says, "We're all in this together," and he believes he and I are both insane people. He's the only person I've ever thought, "Oh, THERE'S my husband!" about. The manager takes us to a different room while his wife comes with a broom to sweep the water out.

We're tired, but we strip-search the mattress corners. I find splinters and wood chips buried in its surface. I tell him,

"When we were kids, we stayed in a hotel with some family friends once. The boys found a bunch of porno mags under a mattress. My mom wanted to burn the place down." Michael asks me to look at his corner, and there are bugs, or pieces of them. Thorax, legs, antennae, heads. Body parts, spread open.

Michael's mother had nine miscarriages before he was born. He almost, or briefly, had a little brother named Dylan, who was stillborn. I have a dead little brother also named Dylan, but mine lived twenty-one years. Michael tells me the difference between he and I is that he's obsessed with death because he's afraid to die, and I'm obsessed with death because I want to.

We both look at the bug anatomy like, "We can't stay here." Even though he's never had a car and hates the road after twenty years of touring, Michael wants to drive. "Are those lights in our lane?" he asks. Two soft yellow globes speed toward us before I understand what they are, and Michael swerves us out of their path. Neither of us are sleeping tonight.

He has a friend with a house in Yucca Valley. Nobody's home, but an old bandmate texts us the code to get in so we can crash. The wine we just bought is half empty when I take it out of the car. I finish it while Michael opens a bottle of gin. A massive, lopsided orange moon comes up over the hills. I say it looks like the lumpy back of a baby's skull. "The baby is nursing, and the sky is its mom's tit."

The next morning, a roadrunner creeps up to take an egg from the nest two doves made above the porch.

Stop Me if You've Heard This

Little excited me more than going to school without panties when I was in kindergarten because you were supposed to wear panties, and I didn't want to. As rules go, it was easy to resist because the resistance was easily hidden. Just keep the hem of your dress yanked down to your sneakers while you sit and don't go down the slide today.

It's weird to talk about sex and children in the same sentence, but when I was small, I thought about sex constantly. The floors of my classmates' Barbie doll houses became littered with inch-long miniskirts and acid-washed jeans kicked free by rigid plastic legs, briefly warmed in my palms, when I came over to play.

Julianna's mom, with her blonde poodle bangs and her obsession with angels, came into the bedroom and shot her gaze down to my drawing of Scary Spice, seated in a simple blue chair, completely nude but for thigh-high black latex stiletto boots, eyes burning in an exaggerated slant copied from the Gargoyle faces on *Gargoyles.*

"You can't draw things like that in our home," she said, slow and loud and pained. "Maybe in your home. Not here." Her oldest son stared from the dark hallway behind her. In the drawing, Scary Spice's nipples were a pair of short, thin lines.

Not very realistic or flattering, I thought, but I didn't think that was bad enough for Julianna's mom to send me down the street back to my house. I got better at drawing nipples.

Twenty years later, I do standup for the first time at Thee Parkside, where six years prior I got a concussion at a Banner Pilot show with Nick, a crust punk artist who once photographed each individual Dorito from a bag of Doritos to make a triangular photo zine. I tell one joke about the concussion, and later repeat it, which is the joke, then another joke about wanting to fuck Scary Spice in my childhood. The joke is that I brag to the audience about being sex positive since I was a little girl, and the joke is listening as they react to that information.

I met Nick during a show I played at a co-op in Santa Cruz where everyone was dressed up as comic book characters and the walls were papered with rights you should know and Barbie doll parts, woven into yarn-bombed nets of color, dangled and danced from the banana trees. With tall stiletto boots like Scary Spice's, I stumbled over empty cans, dressed as Catwoman in a gray spandex turtleneck dress and mask made of little boys' black boxer briefs from Goodwill. I'd cut eyeholes out of its cloth butt cheeks and stuffed and stitched each tiny leg into perky cat ears. Nick left for cigarettes and came back with tinfoil, becoming a Silver Surfer who shed silver after each drink.

We played spin the bottle and nodded out in cushioned corners together under early coast light. We were children as we snuck out to the treehouse with the castle facade, as he removed his dental floss-stitched jeans and said, "I want to lick your pussy until you come," children as we smothered each other's rushes of breath with sticky hands to avoid waking the stranger in the loft above us, and children through the foggy breakfast punctuated by his camera snaps the next day, while for six minutes on YouTube we watched Keith David resist wearing Roddy Piper's sunglasses.

Best Eyes

I don't know what came first: the sexualizing or the sex. My mom says I was boy crazy since I was born, that I flirted with my pediatrician before I could speak very well, batted my eyes and said, *Dot Obeeskee, are gonna gimme shot?*

When I was three, she put me in a tiny swimsuit, gave me a pile of chemical cloud curls and a wet cherry pout, and entered me into a swimsuit pageant for children sponsored by Hawaiian Tropic suntan oil. I think I remember parts of it. The view of the seated crowd from the stage and the hiss of their murmuring, programs fluttering, and cameras flashing. My mother took home three trophies that the judges awarded to my body, one bigger than me and with a gold plastic disc that said *Best Eyes.*

I imagine walking up to the moms and grandmas in the crowd, in my three-year-old shape, to tell them this display of soft, newly formed children is sick, sexual, but the moms and grandmas balk and snort. They think we're cute and our youth extends their own. They think that I'm the one sexualizing it, being weird. Maybe I am. Even this made-up version of me doesn't have the language to tell them she'll always feel exposed, doesn't know the difference between being consumed and being seen.

Hawaiian Tropic doesn't do children's swimsuit competitions anymore, or adult ones. Evidence of the way things used to be seems to disappear more quickly and more utterly with the internet. It's funny because, growing up, adults kept telling us that everything was forever on the internet, and now we're buried in a pile of refuse that never stops growing, impossible to wade through. On eBay, a collector had the flier for the exact pageant I competed in: *June 20th, 1993 at the Mariott Hotel in San Ramon!!!* with a blue photo of the previous year's winners. *GIRLS - BOYS - BABIES - TEENS. Round crowns for girls.* I wonder if the collector was there. I showed it to my friend Rick because it creeped me out, and he sent me ten bucks so I could buy it. If you want something like *MISS HAWAIIAN TROPIC INTERNATIONAL BEAUTY PAGEANT 1993 BUSTY MIXED CARD SET,* or a rare videotape (only $80) from 1991 called *Heat Wave,* featuring Benny Hill *Performing His Incomparable Comedy,* the seller's got those, too.

The back of the VHS sleeve says, *This video, without a doubt, shows the most breath-taking women in the world. Over 3,500 contests were held around the globe to narrow it down to the 48 finest beauties you will ever see. Wearing the latest beach fashions from Brazil to Greece, these women were filmed with the latest in video technology during a week of beach parties, pool parties, celebrity press parties and of course at THE COMPETION* (misspelling and all).

You will also see behind the scenes preparation, back-stage pressure, and the beach fun that is synonymous with the Miss

Hawaiian Tropic International Beauty Competition. See if you agree with our celebrity judges. To be fair to yourself and these beauties you'll have to watch this over and over again. It'll be tough work, but you'll be glad to do it.

The founder of Hawaiian Tropic died in Daytona Beach not too long ago. I'm not sure what killed him. According to his Washington Post obituary—*Ron Rice, 'Suntan King' who Founded Hawaiian Tropic, dies at 81*—he invented Hawaiian Tropic suntan oil in his garage. In Florida, he saw beautiful women in swimsuits and dreamed of selling them something to cover their bodies in. He dumped a number of liquids, random ingredients, and coconut fragrance oils into a twenty-gallon garbage can, stirring it all together with a broom handle.

His story has a carnival barker echo, not unlike the bootstrapped red-blooded American male success stories you hear from politicians or CEOs. Before all the sex and suntans, he was a folksy Carolina mountain boy, and with a $500 loan from dad, he started selling his oil in 1969. I suppose his story and his success are no more or less real than each other, or the beautiful young women on whose bodies he grew rich.

The real gush of Ron Rice's wealth came when he started promoting his suntan oil with beauty pageants. The first Miss Hawaiian Tropic swimsuit competition was held in 1983. *It was absolutely magic,* Ron Rice said. *I had never seen anything like it. We had every horn dog in the world come in and see the pageant.*

They call Ron Rice the Hugh Hefner of Florida. He was a man with Lamborghinis to spare for friends like Burt Reynolds. The New Yorker obituary, written by Susan Orlean, says, *Curiously, Ron Rice was not a tan man, but, with Hawaiian Tropic, he became the king of tan.* Orlean devotes just two sentences to the Miss Hawaiian Tropic pageants. It feels conspicuously bland. He's always just described as fun. He looked like shit. Why did a guy who looked like him have so many young gorgeous women under his sway? Perhaps the girls didn't diminish themselves in power the way I seem to be doing by asking that, by calling them girls (it's not their problem that I always felt discomfort with the title of woman, or that the avenue for recognition, for contrast, I most frequently stalked was occupied mostly by men). To some of them, he must have been just another mild annoyance to be tolerated for a paycheck, or at least, for the exposure.

Maybe I'm projecting self-doubt onto these beauty contestants the way others project their fantasies. Or in some absurd way, there is a taint of jealousy. . . no, worse, entitlement—the feeling of having missed a monkey bar. I briefly had proximity to this big confirmational kind of beauty, but I was only three, which is one of those humbling thoughts that gives you the relief of laughing at yourself. I grew up hearing more kind than unkind things about my appearance, but viewed both with suspicion and believed neither. Even as a hypothetical, beauty's touch lingered and became an ever tightening chokehold, a reminder that *you don't look right and that means something.*

There's no mention of the Little Miss Hawaiian Tropic contests on the Hawaiian Tropic Wikipedia or website. My dad still talks about how angry he was that my mom entered me. Even she realized something was off when a member of the audience waved a twenty-dollar bill at us, the pre-schoolers on stage. There's a video from 2008 on YouTube. The girls look the same age as I was, some with neon colored swimsuit bottoms stretched tight over diapers whose white edges peek out like lace frills.

Marla Maples, the second wife of President and former Miss Hawaiian Tropic celebrity judge Donald Trump, was once a Miss Hawaiian Tropic contestant. There are women who collect beauty titles from among many categories of beauty queen, some I've never heard of before. In addition to Miss Hawaiian Tropics, they are also Miss Hooters, Maxim cover models, Playboy centerfolds, MMA ring girls, WWE Divas, Miss International Israels and Miss Suprainternational Israels, and contestants on a British reality TV show where American porn stars take acting classes and perform classic English drama in the West End.

I wonder if drawing money through the image or idea of one's beauty feels like power, the way that the performance of any labor may confer some kind of power. Collective power, certainly. But the other kind, that draws itself from exploitation rather than work, fills the negative space like noxious gas. So many beauty queens seem to die in their thirties and forties. Half Ron Rice's life or less. Suicides, overdoses. Murdered by husbands. Bodies broken for what? Trying to earn a living?

Maybe we want it to be for something beyond that. An aesthetic ideal. A confirmation of the sense and symmetry in our artificial systems, against which our deep animal bones thrash, that their bodies can bestow upon us supplicants. Maybe the root of this jealousy is in the fear that my body isn't a material resource in the same way, that I lack the kind of body or, really, commitment to the body, that can make me money or make someone else wealthy in this particular line of work. All we have in this life are our bodies, for others to make money off of. I know this. So where did this lack-shaped hole come from?

Again and again, from the pediatrician to classmates and teachers and older guys in bands and boyfriends and their best friends and girl-strangers and my friends, I fumbled blind for understanding expressed as desire or vice versa. Anyone who looked in my direction must be a trophy-bearer. We must either give or receive. We must exist in transactions.

I leapt off a barn roof when I was sixteen for a movie some guys at my high school were making. One of them showed me once how to fall, turned his body to land on the plastic-coated mattress below and bounced back up with long cowboy boot strides. I had no fucking idea what I was doing. I just went for it, stepped off, and felt like I was floating. The fall was nice. The mattress slid out under me and my ankle took most of the weight as I hit the ground. Tingling sharp numbness masked it, but there had to be pain, because I felt like I was going to throw up. Embarrassed and confused, I shot up and limped around. *No I'm fine. I'm fine.* I couldn't see what I was looking at. The guy's parents gave me horse ibuprofen and horse tranquilizers. I was so ashamed of getting it wrong. They weren't filming when I fell, so it's like nobody saw.

My hair was always in my face. Long black and brown bushy curtains. I needed a haircut for that same never-completed movie, and asked my younger sibling Chayo, who cut it too short on accident. I told them it was no big deal because I could hear them crying through our shared bedroom wall, and I tried to get it fixed at a Supercuts and left with a bowl cut and bangs. My skinny goth boyfriend came over and yelled about my hair until I cried. I kinda liked the cut, though, later. It felt like I could have been a member of the Buzzcocks in an alternate universe, and I told myself that meant something.

It was a relief when, later that year, I had to start wearing glasses. I loved having something to hide behind.

I was on a date with someone else when I met Michael. He wanted to see Michael's band on their tour from Seattle because Michael was one of his favorite artists. As soon as Michael entered the bar, we were pulled to each other. He slammed a beer on the table, sat down, and that was it. To be so easily beheld and opened up there with my date watching was intense and unsettling. He said, *What's your story?* Irresistibly, I emptied myself to him.

He came back a couple months after that, stayed for a week. The first night we spent together, I lay on top of him, fixated on the patch of hair nested in his clavicle. He lifted my face to his and said, *You're the kind of person I could develop real feelings for,* in a sort of heavy, troubled voice. I wrinkled my nose and said, *What does that mean?* He answered, *I was interested in you right away. Because of the way your eyeballs look.* I knew he didn't mean it the way the toddler bikini contest judges did. He meant how I peer through them. I knew it because I saw him, too, in the way his sad Paul McCartney eyes did their looking.

The second night I spent with Michael, I purposely left my face and hair undone, wore leggings and a long old purple flannel shirt. I wanted him to want me for anything but my body, my appearance, but it's bullshit because I also wore a delicate lace thong, peachy and sand-colored, and the idea entered me from everywhere and nowhere while I undressed. *Actually, will you take my panties off?*

It thrilled me. I'd never asked anyone to do this before. He looked at me like he was praying, like he had understood a sound from heaven's frequency, and said *Yes* with a capital Y. He took the lace in his big hands and slid the underwear down my thighs, his fingertips skimming the surfaces of my knees, the contours of my long calves. Hovering between Michael and my bed as if on a cloud, between being touched and being undressed, I felt bodiless and beautiful.

After that week we spent splashing in the mess of our big love, Michael went back to Seattle. We struggled to make sense of the parting. *What if this is real?* he asked before I drove him through rain to the airport. *What am I supposed to do?* I told him, *It's real,* and told myself, *It's so real that I bet most people go their whole lives never feeling it. Holy shit I'm so lucky I got that for even a week. I can do anything, now. As long as I live I'll be happy because someone saw me, once.*

Michael and I saw other people and didn't see each other for five years. We were far apart, then, in more than physical distance. By the time we reconnected, we were living even further apart than before, but other distances between us had closed. I twisted and pleaded my body into pitiful but earnest imitations of centerfold poses and sent Michael photo after poorly lit photo. I begged for videos of him making himself come, with sound. I wanted him to know I saw him, and heard him, too.

Now I believe the trick is not so much to see, but to look, first. I look at him, still. I press play. I keep looking. I train my eyes on him, and the small vision of his body begins to alter my breath. I occupy my body, fill and expand beyond it.

A problem I have with being an individual is the difference between perceiving and looking: what are we actually seeing? Bodies or dollar signs? Desire or conditioning? It is mortifying to be seen, as anyone who's sick to death of how we talk when we talk on the internet has heard. Do I assume too much when I say we must all want it in some way? Maybe we don't really know what it is we want, or what it is we are winning when some other human body takes us in, or if we'd still want it, if we knew.

Several women sued Ron Rice for sexual harassment. You might be thinking, *Oh, shocking*. Rice denied everything, settled out of court with one woman and dragged another for six more years until the judge decided he wasn't liable for damages. He sold Hawaiian Tropic to Playtex in 2007, made over eighty million, and then someone else got it from Playtex when they bought Playtex, or another group bought it from the next guy. You know how it is.

After divorcing his first wife, Ron Rice married a former Hawaiian Tropic beauty queen twenty-five years younger than him named Darcy LaPier. At their wedding, they had a carriage drawn by a spotted Appaloosa whose mane and tail were dyed vibrant pink. They drank champagne from what was supposed to be that same goddamned garbage can he mixed all the coconut shit in. This man loved his garbage can.

Within two years, Darcy left him for Jean-Claude Van Damme, who broke it off with his bodybuilder wife for her, and it turned out she never divorced her first husband, so Ron annulled their marriage but raised a daughter with her anyway (child support, no alimony). Then she left JCVD for the founder of Herbalife and JCVD remarried his first wife, and Darcy's Herbalife guy OD'd and died a year later. Now

Darcy has another husband and all these children of successful men, and she lives on a ranch in Oregon where she has made herself over into a star rodeo barrel racer. I sort of smile, imagining her.

Not long after Hawaiian Tropic's Hooters-esque restaurant venture launched and crashed in sexual assault lawsuits, the suits running the brand realized that, since women were their target market and primary consumers, they should appeal to those women instead of appealing to increasingly dated projections of American straight male fantasies. With their new website featuring unretouched models, Hawaiian Tropic sells wellness, a contemporary spin on desirability that is attainable for every body (as long as that body carries money).

I wonder what the company refers to when they describe making products in *the spirit of the islands.* Something about freedom from restriction or responsibility, I guess (so free that they freely associate with islands that appear nowhere in Rice's history). They still claim to be in pursuit of beauty, only now it is *the beauty and joy in all things: our skin, ourselves, our communities, our planet.* This is why they *proudly make products that are free from oxybenzone and octinoxate.* Those things bleach and kill coral reefs. Hawaiian Tropic even rejects bleach now. Gone, disposed of, are the luminescent bottle blondes who once bore their beauty for the brand.

Ron Rice founded another skincare company before he died. Habana Brisa, or Havana Breeze. The company launched recently and their *About Us* mentions the trash can and exotic ingredients. Then their man's whole history is boiled down to *Ron founded Hawaiian Tropic and grew it to become an $8B global brand - #2 in the world, which was sold in 2007 to big industry.* The rest of it is a cloud of feel-good messaging like *reef-friendly. Environment. Locally owned. Trust. Integrity.*

Above it all a banner blares, *Developed by Ron Rice, legendary founder of Hawaiian Tropic.* No mention of beauty queens, the golden bodies that carried his product, or of the small stumbling child bodies following in their wake, or of the lives cut short by big business. His body never sold a single bottle of suntan oil.

Mind Field (2009) Triptych

I. "John Henry Split This Heart," Songs: Ohia (Steve Berra)

Jake moves to our block with his stuttering kickflips in sixth grade. He's tall and has the same name as one of the Animorphs, so he's perfect. I try to skate for his attention, but I can't stomach the way the board rolls out from under me, the unbalancing, so I start learning guitar because he has one. Soon I'm writing my own songs, and I don't mind when he asks me to teach him how to play his beautiful girlfriend's favorites. In eighth grade, he introduces me to some high school guys he skates with. *They're coming over to play guitar so I think you should come,* he says. *I feel like you will fall madly in love.* I wear a skirt I made with my grandma and an Alkaline Trio shirt I cut up and stitched tight to Jake's house, where Bobby, with long blond nineties metalhead hair and shy blue eyes, riffs quietly. I think Bobby is cute, but mostly I'm aware of Jake's bed and comforter under my legs. My desire to know Jake intimately is eventually quelled by knowing him better, but I still wear shoes you're supposed to skate in.

Years later, I'm nineteen and working at Jamba Juice with Alex, one of the sweet punks I'd met while slamming around at Three Oaks or smoking Black & Mild spliffs in the creek during summer breaks. He skates, too, in sharp, fierce movements that make me think, *Shark.* One night after we close, he and his girlfriend Kayla, who together are one of those eternally married couples, take me to some house party where I see Bobby from Jake's room. Bobby stares with pale blue eyes while I play and sing old Alkaline Trio songs on someone's guitar, the early stuff we both like, but somehow it's another guy's tongue that ends up between my legs at the end of the night, and it gives me the feeling of having misunderstood directions somewhere.

The thing with Bob is sweet—two Bay Area babies raised in the shadow of the Battle of the Bay, we get together between our two Spring birthdays, and we argue outside Oakland Coliseum in a way that feels bizarrely loving, like how we fuck in a way we're positive means what older people mean when they can say without cringing that they've made love—but it feels like an anchor before I'm ready to want anchoring. The first time we break up, I tell him my love for him (or maybe I mean my ability to feel happy; even now I'm unsure of the difference) is *like a lightbulb that won't turn on*, and I don't know why I'm only lit up about him part-time. He's lit up like crazy about me, with an intensity that burns, something I shrink from as if it were fury. He's angry too, bitter that he fucked up his knee and can't skate anymore.

I hook up with a friend or two and he hooks up with a friend of his who has what I assume everyone means when they say *a perfect body,* and I simultaneously forget and recall, conjure and obliterate, all the times Bobby made me feel beautiful, like a babe, when he said even my vagina was pretty and that I should keep the beard on it, when he called me *shoog,* and I know he'll get back with me if I want to, so on Halloween he comes to my apartment and I get him back. I find his friend's Tumblr where she writes about how upset she is that Bobby chose me instead of her again, and I think, *Good.* And this thing of ours flares and flashes; flaming white as the C&H sugar sign at night, as the twin swooping bolts on his Janoskis.

II. "Crumble," Dinoaur Jr. (Mikey Taylor)

Alex and Kayla bring Tony, who skates earnestly, with something like grace in his figure, to a party at Kate's and my apartment. Tony laughs loud and has a killer smile, big straight white teeth. I'm drunk when he introduces himself and I howl, *Wow, you have great teeth!* Kate thinks he's hot, so I don't examine my curiosity about him, and I don't know that this same party is his first attempt to come out from a long period of isolation following an army stint in Afghanistan. As the party winds down and shapes start smearing, Tony and Alex go fucking around in the skatepark across the street. Tony stumbles, eats shit, and breaks off his two front teeth in the bowl. I learn about it the next day from being tagged in a picture of him, grinning like a young Tom Savini displaying his own fucked up special effects makeup, and I'm horrified, like I cursed his teeth. Bobby or Alex reassures me, *It's fine, he's got that army insurance.*

Bobby connects me with his best friend Cory, who skates with a kind of sleepy fluidity, because we are both starting to write. I ask Cory if Bobby will like the bootleg *Photosynthesis* and *Mind Field* DVDs I found for his birthday, and he says, *He'll like anything you get him.* I start seeing Cory around the community college campus, and I like his cold indifference and the high contrast thrown in my face when it suddenly evaporates into interest, when the beetle black eyes stay a little too long on mine. Our emails and swapped stories get longer, less fictional, more sexual. I romanticize his addictions, tragedies and traumas, his love for the *clack-clack* of wheels over asphalt equally, imagining them as high towers that keep him ideologically and creatively pure—familiar, like when he tells me he recognized my mom in NA because he recognized me in her, and she tells me a young man approached her after a meeting and said rather than asked, *You're Lauren's mom*—untouchable, in a way that feeds my fearful need to be in constant pursuit of, rather than sitting in one place with, a person.

Bobby's ever-increasing rage toward me is probably driven by my growing antipathy toward him, which makes me feel like shit. But I'm sick of him calling me a bitch when we fight, sick of feeling like he's right when he calls me pretentious, and the lightbulb shuts off when, in Cory's backyard, he tells a story about a girl they know who *let a bunch of guys run a train on her*, and I'm like, *Maybe she had a great time, what's the problem?* I feel for Cory's eyes with my periphery as Bobby explains, *A key that can open any lock is a great key. But a lock that opens for any key…*

I break up with Bob again, and the writing between me and Cory spills over into text messages. He says I'd be a good wife for him. I've never had finesse. I say things like, *Wouldn't this Beach Fossils song be perfect to fuck to?* I think about the first time I heard someone say all punk songs are three chords or fewer, and how boundaries and simplicity are good. It must be that sick pleasure feeling like pressing on a freshly stinging peeled scab to push the blood back in and to feel the underskin that can't be felt otherwise, when I withdraw and wait for him and he doesn't say anything back for a while. Years, sometimes. I keep trying to twist it into a lesson about patience and love; I'm like a dumb puppy.

III. "Kids of the Black Hole," The Adolescents (Anthony Van Engelen)

Cory's telling me to elope with him in Vegas, and fades away—it was Fadeaway or Faderade, the Gatorade-vodka combo Tony christened the night I played solo at the anarchist co-op in the middle of a cornfield in Napa when Bob wagged his crutch at me with jealousy and Tony puked, head highway-out, on the side of my car—and comes back to talk about his regret for not letting himself fall in love with me, and nothing, and *congratulations homie,* and *thanks.* Tony and I spend more time together, and there are a few grayed-out attempts to connect bodies, but his expectation or predictability rubs me wrong. They always talk about music, the best bands in skate videos, and they always talk about the sweat, too. Having sweaty balls and asses and dicks from skating.

There was a day at Pismo Beach, or maybe Stinson, with all three of them, when I was still dreaming of a serious cute future with Bob and feeling Cory's eyes on me in the sand and leaning comfortably into Tony's bright bobbing energy. Too loud and too bright, laughing loud and drinking louder. I rocked between them all, carried on their waves. I'm freest when I'm one of them, or when I can pretend to be. Like rolling over concrete, no, like flying above it. Your stomach before you plummet. The best part.

Landing, then. Losing touch with Bob while he befriends my brother, who I also lose touch with, and lashing out at Bob because I hate how he asks if it's a joke when he learns of my brother's suicide, and even though I broke up with him twice before I'm scared to see him with his young girlfriend who used to have a crush on my little brother at my little brother's funeral. The fight with Tony, after he rescinds his offer to take my mind off Dylan's death by spending a weekend together in San Francisco, because his girlfriend, after combing through our emails, believes we're cheating, and she commands us to stop speaking to each other or she'll feed Tony's dick to our children. Cory reappears and writes, but doesn't say out loud, that I should meet him in Italy, that I'm sacred, that he loves me and will always be in love with me, and I don't know if it's that I'm scared to be a fool when it turns out he doesn't mean it, or that my own disbelief is enough to make any *us* unreal, but his words hurt and confuse, and even though I think I want to, I never say them back because, in some ideologically and creatively pure, untouchable way, I feel ran through.

My Brother Doesn't Show Me His Head

We're leaving the concrete house with the cacti, the orange tree, and the tree we thought was a peach except for the hard teardrop fruits and manic pink flowers that fell off it. It's right that Allen should take the cat. He found her, scratchy-voiced kitten wet from rain, near the Dollar Tree dumpster. I couldn't name her. She was Gatita when I was happy and Cat more often.

The first night, Gatita slept in the bed with us, a little knot. In a corner, darker than the room's darkness, a figure stood, edges vibrating.

Terror pumped heat into my still body. Gatita sat before it, visible by white toes and the golden glow wrapped like a pipe cleaner around her silhouette, staring it down. The figure reached to take me, but she kept it there.

My mom had night terrors, too. When I was young, she'd talk about the devil holding her up by the ankles, and how she saw her brother walking by and tried calling out to him for help, but her lips were glued and her body paralyzed. When she described it to me her eyes went wide the way mine do when something tries to get out but can't.

Once, I visited Papi's house and fell asleep in the middle of the day, thinking about my then-boyfriend's best friend Cory. Dream landscape bled into former teenage bedroom around me, flat on the grass of the green couch. Cory's rottweiler licked my cheek and asked me with his body to play. Cory stood apart, observing through an unmoving face. I tried to make my arm move, couldn't. My ears heard the soft moan struggling to become words like *I can't move* and *Help me.*

I'd so filled the blank months before Allen and I met with cum and pills and river dirt after my younger brother's death that I felt ready to meet him when I did. But my brain is unchanged from the moment Dylan blew his to pieces. So he's getting the cat. He found her, and he can take care of her.

Abuelita saw duendes in her house, or maybe they were aliens, something she called visitors. I've read about poltergeists and dark things that hitch to human life, shards of cosmic nonmatter that trauma or mental disorder or malicious unknowable things welcome into your folds to seep or bubble to the surface at will.

I've never calculated the sleep lost every night, every week, every year for as long as I can remember trying to sleep, but I heard sleep deprivation can shorten your lifespan by fifteen percent. It seems to me a lifespan can't be determined until it ends. They say it takes way more time sleeping than the original, lost amount to make up for the loss. In this sense, I get why death is the big sleep; all the time you've spent awake, consciously alive, how long would it take to recover from that?

When Dylan killed himself, I was sleeping on the floor of Becky's Midtown one-bedroom. Her lease ended, and I found us a cheap apartment in a rotting Victorian on a part of the grid that was cooled by the American River. On our first morning there, I carried pizza boxes down the dim stairwell out to the alley dumpster and saw a shape that almost glittered, blue and green, near the dumpster's wheel. A peacock, dead with open eyes, tail feathers hacked down to white, stiff, stems.

The curve of its neck, the liquid of its eyeballs, made something in my chest crack open and dribble out. I thought Becky, who kept an owl in our freezer, should see the peacock. I brought her to the alley, where an old man now stood, smoking. Through his cigarette, he said, *That thing is cursed.*

Becky removed the bird's head and wings from its body, to preserve them. She entered the kitchen pale from twisting and cutting its corpse apart with dull garden shears. Later, she painted me topless and cutting apples, for an art show. Alone of all the portraits that covered the high wall, mine fell, glass shattered.

The peacock parts stayed in a box filled with cornmeal in the narrow back stairwell for weeks. Some nights, I felt my calves being grabbed. Others, I woke up with scratches.

My more spiritual comadre Blanca told me Dylan sent Gatita to stop the sleep paralysis. I was lucky for the two-year reprieve, and I don't dread the return of the figures in shadow. The paralysis is the worse part. It's in my brain. It leaks into daytime and squeezes my tongue. When the body is in motion, I'm knocked loose in it.

Papi was alone in the house where Dylan had once lived, so in the days after he died, I stayed there. Asleep in the guest room that used to be mine, my eyes opened to yellow light coming through the half-closed door.

Dark movement in the hall set off the reptile alertness that shrieks until it understands what it is seeing. Dylan's knee, then his long shin. All black. The rest of his thin body slid out of the impossible space where a wall should be. He lurched through the doorway as though tugged from the belly.

Fury radiated from his obscured figure. As a kid he was gentle, sensitive, but when his temper exploded it settled in layers over everything. He opened the back of Chayo's head with one swing of a PVC pipe at three years old because they'd knocked over his Legos. Papi pressed a shoprag to Chayo's skull while driving us to the emergency room. Blood soaked the blue rag red. I thought, *It should be purple.*

Dylan crept forward to show me his final wound. I hadn't seen his body since it lived. Strapped down with open eyes, I watched as his head began to roll toward me. We froze in a moment where everything that hasn't happened yet was visible.

He withdrew his head, stepped backward into the hall, and disappeared. The light was still on.

Maybe it won't work for you. Maybe you are too smart or too cemented in your physicality. Or you've run your brain through more powerful substances than I have. But if you want to try to leave your body the way I did as a kid, here's how:

First, stand in front of a mirror. Somewhere that feels blank and big, a little unfamiliar. Maybe your bathroom at night, with only bare traces of light, or a hanging mirror that you drag to a different corner.

Stare into your reflection's eyes as they stare into yours. Now think about your name. You can say it in your head, but saying it out loud, even in that kind of whisper where you barely move your lips and your teeth freeze, like you don't want anyone, not even the reflection, to know you're talking, is better. Repeat it until it becomes a funny-sounding word with no meaning, the way all words do, until you reach the end of that word's tether to your consciousness, and realize that nothing, not even this word, means anything.

*

When I look at this body, it is made of missing pieces: dead hollows and grooves, pulsing reds, jagged edges like broken glass crowning a wall.

"Yeah, there's a name for that," says someone, maybe a nursing assistant, in a videochat while skimming his DSM. "It's a type of OCD called excoriation disorder."

I'm only in this call to get my drugs refilled after being out for two months. To stifle the brain's noises. Beneath the desk, I feel my hands' unevenness and try to peel it even, but I rip too far. It's a ritual that's gone unbroken for as long as I can remember. The stab of reactive nerve pain in my belly telling me to stop is part of it too, the tattoo of being alive.

Later, Michael squeezes my rolling hips and groans, "You're the hottest bitch I've ever seen." I am insane with love. I lick his throat and will remember the taste of his sweat until I'm dead.

It's one of the only things that puts me back in the body, since I fled from it by accident when I was six.

*

I don't remember what made me do this. But I remember the instant I understood that the name Lauren Lavín meant nothing, Lauren Lavín's face, nothing, Lauren Lavín's long hair and scars up and down her limbs, nothing. My tongue tingled, then numbed. The face in the mirror dimmed and the bathroom dissolved.

I was nowhere and everywhere. The entirety of Lauren Lavín's life raced ahead of her, laughably microscopic compared to how big I was.

Whenever I take psychedelics, I am unimpressed by the trip and wonder if I did something irreparable to my developing brain in the bathroom mirror.

I did things that seemed to put me back in the body, too. Bit holes in the pads of fingers, gouged skin from ankles and knees. Scratched flesh until spots appeared and dug to find out what was under the spots. Burned patches away with big pink erasers.

One of the earliest things I identified as Mexican in a way that I related to, flipping through one of Papi's books on the floor, was the Aztecs cutting hearts and blood from people as offerings for Huitzilopoctli. I drew crooked temples with brick-colored crayon streams down their steps. Beautiful black-haired priestesses and corpses.

A police chopper spits and sputters over the neighborhood for an hour, and I can't concentrate. Sometimes I think the best way to die is getting eaten by a large animal. Like, fill yourself with lidocaine and heroin and let a puma kill you, live off you. If the body is a cage, I think there is still a difference between hating it because you wish it were a nicer cage and hating it because you wish you weren't trapped inside.

During our first big love affair, Michael said, "I like that you talk about your body and brain like they're separate entities."

"I do?"

"All the time. Like they communicate with two cans and some string."

*

Although Papi was from Veracruz, where Cortez incinerated Spanish ships in his devotion to invasion, we went to Playa del Carmen, where one of my white mom's uncles had owned a small hotel since it was a tiny fishing village. Then, the town swelled with resort hotels, McDonald's and TGI-Friday's. Great Uncle Bill prospered and let us stay there cheap.

My parents were divorced, and I don't know why Papi came. His distaste for the once-beautiful, now overrun tourist trap was thick like the humid air, and I breathed it in. Darker-complexioned than my siblings, sometimes the target of jokes my uncles said were harmless, I crawled in my skin, perturbed by the way white people were waited on by Indians in Indian country, aware of my ultimate location on the American tourist side of that equation, and squirming with the sensation that I belonged with, to, nobody, nowhere.

My mom took us to the part of the beach where Europeans and Americans were topless and sometimes bottomless, so she could tan her enormous breasts. She poked my arm and nodded at a sunbather to her left, saying, "Look, it's a pirate's dream: a sunken chest." I flattened myself facedown into the sand and didn't know yet that hers were mostly silicone.

I was eleven and could stay out until midnight, sneak beers, and smell the ocean the way it was supposed to be, not like the ear-stinging beaches in Northern California. I found my dad, and he pushed a big silver peso coin into my palm. Its pearl-bright surface was engraved with a woman in pieces whose name I couldn't make out, it was so tiny.

"'Coyolxauhqui,'" he read.

Her tits were angular, nipples pointed down, away from her severed arms and toward her severed legs.

"You put naked dead people on money?" I asked, elated.

"Is more like a novelty," he said in his second language. "The government is always making new kinds of pesos and retiring old ones. Is not worth as much as it says."

All her parts were arrayed in what looked like a beautiful dance. In her tumbling head, her mouth was thrown open as if in ecstasy.

*

A lot of the out of body experiences were not intentional, and I escaped the body for the black endless place again while a man Lauren Lavín invited over to jam hit her in the face, while maybe she asked him to, while he fucked her as she shoved her puke-covered bra out of her dewy field of vision. But I was very much in the body when I became pregnant from a fun party hookup a few years later.

My instinctive first response to seeing the result on the pregnancy test was, "Shit I gotta get an abortion now." Even when my mom pleaded with me to keep it, swatted at my certainty with excuses like, "You don't even have a placenta yet, any drinking or smoking you've done hasn't affected it," and "a baby would be so good for the family right now," nothing flickered in my judgment.

I had detected my pregnancy early and wasn't allowed to abort for at least four more weeks. I wanted it gone immediately. But with a guaranteed end to the experience, it became weirdly easy to feel it fully, to leave it to the body and discover how that made the body feel.

I was glowing, overflowing with life, and it felt good, absolutely, all over. At a wedding, I fucked a friend in a stranger's truckbed even though he was with someone who he married later, and fucked him again that night in his hotel room. Each revolution of my bicycle wheels across flat city streets was *doing* something. When I closed my eyes, I felt it like a small cluster of fireflies.

So it made sense when, amid all my gratitude and certainty, it hurt as much as it did to be spread on my back naked from the pussy down, with the old woman shoving cold metal deep inside me and Kate locking my hand in hers. I was as ecstatic to not be a mother as I was to know that I could be. For maybe the first time I felt something like balanced, truly neutral, even as some girl cried quietly behind a curtain waiting for her drugs to kick in.

*

Google says there are 9,463.53 drops of water in a pint. A clumsy series of calculations leads me to conclude that I've shed 52,195 drops, or roughly five and a half pints of blood.

It's somehow more and less than I thought. In the moment, it is such a small thing.

I picture the pints of blood on the desk in front of me and wonder if it would feel better to have dedicated that amount to something as a sacrifice. Or even to know the reason it's there, outside of me, in the first place. It can feel like a habit, a personality flaw, a bad coping strategy, a symptom of my obsession with imperfections. But seeing the patterns is no trouble at all for an obsessor. Breaking them is.

As a girl in the mirror, if I wasn't speaking my brain out of my body, then I ached with fantasies where I pinched and pulled parts of it like Play-Doh, peeled chunks from my thighs, belly, arms, and stacked them where I thought people wanted them.

As an adult, the fantasies have moved to the brain, where I scrape away the parts that make me grind my teeth to different time signatures all night, until my neck seizes and my jaws crack. The offending tissue is rolled up and flicked into a corner, the remaining dents squished together and rubbed smooth.

I accept a doctor's advice to take NAC for the excoriating. It's not at the usual grocery store where they started locking up ice cream and fish, but they have it at the natural foods co-op where Michael was a cashier before we met. Maybe it helps. Other parts of the body are easily hidden, but I struggle to leave my hands alone.

*

Before Coyolxauhqui was ripped apart, her mother Coatlicue got knocked up miraculously. A ball of hummingbird feathers fell into her dress while she was sweeping a temple. Symbolically, the implication is that an anonymous soldier did the knocking. I read somewhere that it was a similar thing with Mary and Jesus.

Coatlicue wears a skirt made of serpents. In the famous statue of her, heavily fanged snakes coil out of her neck to form a grinning two-mouthed monster-god-head, and from her hands and her pussy, all the parts of her that were wounded, that bled. She wears a necklace of human hearts, hands, and skulls. Her breasts are flaccid, drooping, from nursing her many children. It comforts me to think of fertility and death as somehow un-separate.

When she discovered her mother's pregnancy, firstborn daughter Coyolxauhqui was furious. I'm not sure why she felt that way, but I think I kind of get it. I'm a firstborn, too. She rallied her four hundred brothers, the Centzon Huitznahua, to attack and kill Coatlicue. But the baby bastard Huitzilopoctli leapt fully grown and armed for battle from his mother's womb to slaughter his siblings. He started with his oldest sister, Coyolxauhqui, who had led the matricidal charge.

Huitzilopoctli lopped off her head and threw the body down a gorge where it broke and fell and broke and fell.

*

I apologize to the nail tech for my hands.

"I never get manicures but I'm getting married tomorrow."

A ripple passes over her face, and she suggests a lighter shade than the shimmering pink I panic-grabbed off the wall.

She says, "This will look more natural."

There isn't enough length on these ridged seashell nails for her to even try cutting them. The quicks and cuticles have been scraped away, scarred over, and the soft raw fingertips bubble out. I say sorry over and over and try not to stare at the perfect, groomed women having their feet massaged by women who they glance at over phones, to inspect their work.

Through layers of plastic and warm paraffin wax, she rubs my hands, tells me to put coconut oil on them every night. I want to, but I don't.

*

On the trip where I got the Coyolxauhqui coin, Great Uncle Bill got blitzed at dinner and looked at my mom with eyes that I knew already by then were not for younger family.

"You're a slut," he said to her and grinned across the table. "You're a puppy slut from Hell."

The knuckles in my small brown hands went white around a knife. He didn't notice, already on to the next thing which was his passionate idea for saving the world.

"It's overpopulated. You see it here. You can run over a man in the street, and no one cares, bang, instantly a dozen babies to replace him."

Papi wasn't there. I tried to catch my mom's eye, like, *Your uncle is talking about us.*

"What we really need is a serious virus. Something to, bang, take out 90% of the population. Then we get our own island."

Oh, he thinks he's talking about us, I realized, looking at my artificially blonde mom and her relatives, *but, bang, he's talking about them.*

*

How come whenever someone has tried to look at or capture me, it feels like having parts of the body stolen and put back warped?

Well, it doesn't, not every time. Not with Michael. Something comes back to me changed after I meet him, and I like the slow spread of unfurling bloom that results, that continues.

Michael doesn't think it's right to compare the quiet ritual of self-mutilation to an offering, or to martyrdom, or even to self-flagellation, which might be the closest analog now that I think of it. Like any other impulse, it is merely an extension of the ego part of the body that didn't exist before and won't exist after.

I leave the things that are of the body to the body. In a

way, I like that marriage is mostly about ownership and property.

"I want to belong to you in every way," I tell Michael. "Even on paper."

Please have this body while it lasts.

We agree our marriage will be about each moment, a decision we make present to present, and in that way, no matter how or when it ends as all marriages and things do, it will have been forever, complete.

Every other letter or so hurts to type. I keep stopping to wipe my hands inside the pockets of my jeans. The swollen shiny red skin where cuticles should be is perpetually ringed in vibrant blood.

"Stop it," he says and closes a big hand over mine.

I gush with gratitude for him. I can't believe how lucky I am to have someone care about me this much. As soon as his back is turned, I find another jagged edge that needs me to bleed it smooth.

Zero is a Seashell

My husband and I are hangover-late to Robert and Starla's garage sale and hungry to see the house they bought. We got married earlier this year, so I say *husband* a lot when I mean *Michael.*

All the most beautiful parts of the house come from Robert's hands and Starla's head. Drying blood-colored window frames with rippling glass that splinters the late summer light. Open-angled shelves for Starla's paintings. They own so much space. Michael and I exchange smiles that mean *Damn, we're never going to live like this, are we?*

Robert says, *How's not drinking?* to my husband, who's gone twenty days, except one, without. *Right now, it's okay,* Michael says. Like the first few underwater seconds of held breath.

No one comes to the yard sale.

Around back, Robert and his stepson Z have built a DIY Slip 'N Slide down their steep backyard hill: a seventy-foot blue tongue of staked tarps clamped to ladder railings, its tip a curved ramp above an inflatable pool. Looking down its length, I feel gravity's tug.

*

Steepness and height didn't rattle me when I was young. We lived near a park dominated by a massive concrete slide. At its base, there were always cardboard scraps to slide on. We never brought our own. It was exhilarating, hissing over smooth cement until your speed approaching the end forced your eyes shut.

My younger siblings Chayo and Dylan were born one year and one day apart. When they turned seven and six, their birthday party swelled with children who crashed into and bounded away from each other beyond the slide's shadow and screamed and giggled up and down its pyramid steps.

*

No kids are around now, so we go to a bar for lunch. Michael sits apart from us, crushing it at Ms. Pacman. Something between worry and anticipation wells up as I swallow my gin. He announces, *I've decided to have a drink.* It is relief, like falling. He wants it to be different this time. Later, he says, *I thought about taking a secret shot but wanted to tell you instead, because you're my wife.*

When we return to the house, some wigs are gone. A few dollars unwrinkle in the money jar, and Z drives back from his teenage errands ready to slide. He inflates and fills the sagging pool as Starla and I wobble inside and explains, *There's no way this pool will burst, it is physically impossible.* We shriek at the water our bodies splash over the electric pump he is waving and teasing us with.

Robert and Star's younger kid isn't around, but has made their presence felt in kiddo handwriting, in dust on the car outside, that says, *The end is nier.*

*

Near the slide's highest steps, I painted flowers and Spider-mans on younger kids' faces. Eventually Justin, a friend of a brother of a friend, climbed up with a girl whose bobbed hair was electric box-dye red. They were older, seemed like boy-friend and girlfriend. She rolled a Pepsi can down the slide and chirped, *Go get it!*

They were both grinning when Justin flew down in pur-suit. He reached, slid wildly off course, and spun with his arms out. His twirling slowed, then he stopped at the bottom and didn't move. The party sounds receded. Strange to see all those people and hear nothing.

From my perch, I watched a frantic man—Justin's father?—pump his hands on the boy's chest, creating waves across the pale skin of his exposed belly.

*

Further up the hill, Robert cuts my husband's hair. He flits, slices and rearranges with the same delicate focus he gives Michael's music as an engineer. Seven years ago, when I drove to Seattle from Sacramento to spend the night with Michael, he sent Robert to keep me company until band practice was over. We drank whiskey, talked about my dead brother and his dead father.

Stretched out in Starla's bikini with the 5pm sun beating my skin, I sip a boozy huckleberry something. Not for the first or last time, I feel the space in me, like the empty seashell that is the Maya symbol for zero, where I could grow a child.

Papi says our ancestors influenced Maya writing and math. They knew of zero, knew there was nothing and no anything without that nothing. Michael isn't struggling not to drink, but struggling to drink nothing. To be alive is the moment of hovering between slick blue tarp and re-inflated pool.

*

Justin was twelve when the undiagnosed heart condition killed him on the concrete slide. The only evidence of the incident I can find is in the town's Wiki. Someone wrote, *In the 1990's a kid with a heart condition went down the slide, had a heart attack half-way down, and died. In other words, some caution is occasionally advisable.*

*

After Z squirts yellow Dawn all over the tarp, Robert lets his stepson push him on an inner tube. His foot bangs hard into one of the ladder-rails along the side, and one of the big clamps holding tarp to rail whirls into the air. Michael and I feel its impact through the dirt and wide-eye each other as Robert dips gracefully into the water.

It is a marvel how they land every time. How Robert's thin hands, in his wiry frame that Michael points out *could be Z's in thirty years,* propel this kid, belly down and pointed like Superman, over dish soap and hose water.

I don't breathe as Robert builds speed for Z. I wait for an ankle to snap, a tumble off the ramp, bone, blood, for the pain and fear. I see my husband. Z cruises to the bottom of the slide, flies straight up, and hovers forever above the crooked pool.

The Third Beat

A few days after Dennis died, which was how I learned he'd been out of jail a year, I'm in the desert writing ambient spoken word music with Michael about an artist couple's botched double suicide. Probably the idea for the record came to me on a night where Michael and I held each other in his bed, his eyes watermelon-split with fear of his illness and of dying.

Michael opens his mouth into the tissue-thin desert night air, realizing he knew Dennis because of some old music connection. A snake pulls itself up the hill toward us and, curving around a rock at our feet, feeds its coils into a hole like it's being sucked.

Ian tells me on the phone, That's what punks do, is die. He tells me this because, in our thirties, the deaths of friends are starting to hit different than they used to.

Ben and Heather, the friends hosting us in their desert house, offer true stories—deaths—of their own. It's not a game, more a collecting of fragments that, in the gathered and dug-up pile of rough names and extinguishments, must become enough. In tones of reverence and almost ease, they give us a bandmate who OD'd, and a wild coworker who knew she had terminal cancer but didn't tell anyone until after her arrest, and who died within the year.

I get wasted and tell Michael time isn't real, it's just the way we as beings of matter perceive our own decay—by rudely pinning a label through decomposition's chest. He scoffs and I love him for it.

On our way here Michael, who doesn't drive, swerved my car away from the driver going our way, the wrong way, in our lane, before I understood the large soft yellow lights coming toward us were headlights. The one big hill like a black frozen wave to the west swallows the sun well before sunset and, in the bluing light, I think of Calvin colliding with a parked trailer in the middle of the night, age twenty-five, off the street in Vacaville where I'd lived, and where Dylan had lived. His family asked the hospital to keep his body alive, which they did for a while.

Church social media pages shared pleas for prayers to join those of the family, but in the end, they unplugged Calvin because he'd wanted his remains to be of use, and there was someone to use his heart. I pined bad for him when I was younger and, once we finally did fuck, sometime between my brother's death and his, I was too surprised by the occurrence—unaware even after he'd walked into my room and removed his shirt that he wanted to sleep with me—to know if it was enjoyable. Ian told me recently that Calvin was hammered on that last drive. Refracted through my lens, it becomes a kind of suicide. He wasn't a punk, but it's still like Ian said.

Calvin's family was the religious kind that my brother Dylan wanted. I met him when he was nineteen, and I suspect my apartment, my roommates and I were brief curiosities, escapes from the tight white Christian world that held him, the same one my brother ran hungrily toward. They dated the same girl too, somewhere in that criss-crossing. They're both dead. Calvin isn't his real name. You're not supposed to speak ill of the dead, but we agree on this for the living. I don't have anything ill to say about Calvin.

I'm not sure what the rules are for writing about real people.

Real people name themselves and receive names. Dylan was Alex as a kid because of his middle name (Alejandro). Chayo was Gabby as a kid because of their middle name (Gabriella, with too many l's, to their chagrin). I was never an Angie because of my middle name (Angélica, which I liked correcting people about as a kid because I got to emphasize the "hell").

Calvin and Dylan went to The Father's House. I hate that fucking church. My former babysitter Christy, I assume, still goes. I'm fascinated by her, some lingering awe over the cool and distant Gen X dark-lipped teen version of her that lives in my childhood memory clashing with her current incarnation as Christian wellness influencer-cum-white nationalist militia mommy. I think she has a lot of power that she gives herself, like a name, freely but not without struggle, because she believes it comes from god. I imagine her inhaling it, inflating with it. Does she know she's giving it to herself? Does she know she can?

Days after Dylan died, Christy appeared at my dad's doorstep to say with her whole heart that the devil was in Dylan. Doing evil. Something like that.

We were both like, Okay. And we felt it as rage.

At his memorial service in a small garden chapel, she appeared again, saying Dylan would have wanted all of us to get right with god. The last I had heard, he'd left her church and had been converting to Catholicism. I was indignant, struck dumb by her. I didn't speak at all at his funeral. I should have, maybe, should I have? Why not give myself the power this woman has given herself?

The other thing besides death that Dylan beat me to is walking the Camino de Santiago, which he did alone the same year he was diagnosed with obsessive compulsive personality disorder by the United States Navy and held apart while the others completed basic training. I wanted to be funny in this essay. Dylan was naturally funny in a way that's difficult to describe. He was like a Muppet strung to the black center of the universe.

A lot of funny people destroy themselves. Maybe a lot of people who destroy themselves are funny. During our extended quarantine cohabitating breakup, Allen said that writing comedy changed me for the worse.

Allen doesn't want me to use his name when I write about him anymore, which is his middle name, which he switched to around the time we started dating because his first name reminded him of a certain dominant Western religion devoted to Jesus Christ. Also, his birthday was Christmas Day, which I agree is a little much. Christy, on the other hand, being named for Jesus, must love her name. I imagine she loves her life. Once, she was internet famous for going to a school district meeting and yelling at everybody. Pointing and jabbing beneath her mounds of fluffy hair, she beseeched people to open elementary schools during the pandemic and demanded more than begged, Don't China my America. Disgust and awe intertwined in me and dripped out. I restarted the video again.

I want some of that breath of god shit in me, too. Or maybe that's not the problem, maybe I have it and I'm too much of a pussy to use it. Enough of the theory classes I took at various levels of debt-funded community and state college seeped through the haze around my brain to leave me settled in the idea that words beget thought, and not the other way around.

Retreating from that last relationship, I buried myself deeper into a clumsy ongoing process of befriending Death. I assembled an altar for Santa Muerte, smoked weed at it, left offerings and meditated in front of it, trying either to see things or keep my eyes closed to them, and wrote down whatever I told myself I was seeing. In a way, it's a joke, I guess, to pursue a relationship with Death and, in so doing, kill something, if a relationship is something you can kill (a Jung quote in one of the suicide books I'm reading goes, "Only that which can destroy itself is truly alive"— and to me that sounds like edgelord shit).

The ultrasound printout of the weed lobbyist's aborted almost-baby goes on the ofrenda every year alongside a picture of Dylan as a boy. The days I had to wait before aborting, my pregnant body felt good. The fact that I got knocked up around Dylan's birthday and the due date would have been his death day seemed spooky, if nothing else. Still, I noticed the little electric hum in my body and enjoyed it. I didn't want children with my ex, which I figured meant I didn't want children. Now sometimes I do.

Partly, it's that I wonder if you can sacrifice a part of yourself and live still, to cheat at it, if creation can be anything but a game. The light of long evenings injects Michael's irises with yellow threads in flashed movements that feel un-separate from every moment that hasn't happened yet. I suppose this means some part of me thinks making life, bringing a child into consciousness, would be fun, even though I've seen what can happen. All games end. The gambit of birth-life-death follows comedy's rule of three, which is about making people feel something is funny more than it is about making people laugh. The action is to make a person's lens align with yours for a second. The laugh is the symptom or end result. I guess you could say it's the Death part of the joke.

After Dylan died, I began compulsively transporting into his body at the moment he shot himself. It is easy to say I rejected him in life, that I didn't try to know him for real, because we were alike. Last year, an ancient psychiatrist with an Argentinian accent and a German surname put me, by mistake, on a combination of stimulants and antidepressants that took sixty pounds from me in three months, and my relatively skeletal frame reminded me so much of my brother's that I began to love it. Dylan was a model in his teens. On the way home from a shoot, he was stabbed at a BART station and didn't tell anybody. I found out after he died, in an essay he'd written for school. He described the knife sliding in and out in a way that surprised more than hurt him.

Dylan died holding a rosary with one hand. I never saw the body. I don't know if he did it through his mouth or through the side of his skull. My parents must. Maybe I will ask them about it.

I have never seen where Dylan lived and slept and breathed and did all three of those things for the last time. I sit on his bed in a dark, small room. The wall to my left, the door to my right. I close my eyes right before squeezing the trigger, but still I see a flash behind my eyelids. I am too scared to watch, in the daydreams. I think of Dylan feeling that scared. That is the thing that finally made me cry. Did the clutched rosary mean the last thing he felt was peace, or fright?

It's not like he didn't have agency, or even power. Christy said it was the devil. And who am I to say Christy is wrong? I heard voices a couple times. Not enough to worry about. Once, it was my mother's voice telling me to kill myself, but when I talked about it, I described it as the devil speaking in her voice, because for some reason I thought that would be easier for another person to understand. Maybe it was teenage hormones or one of the things that makes me similar to Dylan. If god is an illusion, then so's the lack of it. We make patterns, and we fill spaces, but I don't know how much we get to decide about when we do those things, except if we decide to do nothing at all, to punch out early.

I'm not interested in questions like, Is suicide genetic? Or, What is the likelihood of suicide if a relative kills himself? Because everything being what it is (a material condition), what difference does it make? I mean that life is itself a material condition, an experience of matter limited by matter and its decay, its full flicker within the boundaries of time. People who ask questions like that aren't interested in keeping other people alive, merely in stopping them from dying at inconvenient times.

My white great-great grandmother Roxana Lynn died in childbirth, and, at her grave, her husband shot himself. There is a photo of him sitting on the tombstone, looking at something far away behind the photographer. In her very early twenties, my mother was engaged to a man and pregnant with his baby. She ended the engagement and pregnancy. I don't know in which order. The man died. She described seeing his identical twin brother years later and got a lost look, which is what they call it when you're unstuck in time. I haven't spoken to my mother in years, but I'm thinking of changing that soon. I'm always thinking of changing it soon.

I also feel unstuck from time, since Dylan's sudden and complete exit. Doug Rice, the teacher whose words ("never marry a mathematician") I used to kill a relationship once, also says you have to take time before you write about something, you can't be that close to it; but don't waste time because it's the only thing you have been given. Nothing I have done in the last few years has been either wasteful or productive, but something in limbo, between.

It is death that is decisive. Suicide is decisive.

I can change tomorrow, I can change the day after that. Maybe I will, probably I won't, and it's impossible to know. A person who kills themself has changed their life. I suppose changing your life is a relative concept.

I'm always thinking of changing it soon.

I'm never closer to my brother than when I'm suicidal, which is one word for that soft, oppressive feeling of being tired with no certainty of rest. There are many other words for it because there are many iterations, soldered into our internal and external systems and wired through precious materials extracted, placed, and consumed with blood. The layers peel back, and there's nothing beyond the veil. Maybe this is what it felt like.

No, this is definitely what it felt like. Maybe feeling like offing yourself isn't the only shared experience I had with my brother. If I write it I have to believe it, to some extent, maybe, if word begets thought.

I remember the day Dylan was born. Each time I replay the memory, I do more damage to it, breaking the dish and sealing it along the cracks, losing water whenever I fill and pour it into myself. I was three years old. Chayo was one year and one day old. I wore a teal dress with pink hibiscus flowers. Before I typed this, the flowers may have been more like birds of paradise, or perhaps white flowers of some other kind, but this is how I will remember them the next time. And Papi was joking with someone, maybe one of my mom's brothers, or her mom, about naming the baby Jake. Or perhaps it was the other way around, them teasing my dad about it, knowing how impossible Jake sounds in his accent, how pulpy and smashed the opening consonant. Dylan was also hard for him.

The room was bright. Dylan had blond curls until he was out of his toddler years and big gray-green eyes. People sometimes followed or stopped our noticeably Mexican Papi, suspecting him of kidnapping someone else's baby. Soon, Dylan was sucking on his middle two fingers until his teeth dug deep, permanently infected sores into their middle two knuckles. He was met with disgust for reacting to the potent fear and volatility in our overlapping childhoods.

We weren't talking much, but he called me from basic training while isolated to tell me he'd stayed up all night folding eighty-something of his bunkmates' bandanas. Sensitive to touch, eager to make others laugh, overwhelmingly loud and fast manners of speaking. Other things we have in common.

Michael is the only living product of many pregnancy attempts and miscarriages (I want to say too many, except I know how it ended) by a mother with the same first name as me, which unfortunately is not a joke, so I explain siblings to him by describing Dylan as a person for whom I was measurably responsible. But how to explain what it is to have been present for his first seconds, and to know where I was during his last? Some stories are short, and some are long. Maybe there is no such thing as a single, complete story. Maybe together they're all complete.

In the last dream I have about him, he's an infant swaddled in gray and blue blankets. The blond curls have returned. He's flanked by our two childhood dogs, including the one who was given away and who, until this dream, I didn't know was dead. They have sockets without eyes. Dylan is so small on the ground and looks exhausted by the circuitry of it all. He was the third baby, the third part of our big existence joke. After the third beat comes laughter, release, and then, quiet.

WHERE THERE USED TO BE RAZORS THERE ARE BARCODED HANGING CARDS

No one keeps picking up at the Safeway [harmacy, which is a typo I'm going to keep. I leave please-help-me-but-don't-judge-me-as-desperate voice messages every two days until I lose count. I keep withdrawing, my husband asking *Are you okay?* No one calls back. *You seem down.*

Today, someone picks up and says my drugs will be ready at two p.m. We get to the pharmacy a couple hours later and join the back of the drug line, which is so long it spans several aisles. Like a bird flock twisting in the sky, it splits for each cart that rattles through it and re-forms. In the distance, one miserable cartoon tornado pharmacist. Michael realizes he'll have to get groceries without me.

Some people give up and leave, but not me, I'm staying. The humiliation of being last in line drains off with each defeated senior walking out. Where there used to be razors there are barcoded hanging cards that you take to the register so another worker can get the razors for you. Time stretches and stretches. With a Safeway worker in line behind me and the camera eye watching above, I put a box of hair removal cream into my coat pocket. Do you know what "shrink" and "throwing" and "facing" mean? Look it up or work at a grocery store.

Michael returns to me carrying a full basket. In the aisle to my left, a Safeway worker who is off the clock and shopping in uniform talks to another Safeway worker who is on the clock and facing a shelf. The older worker who's off says to the younger worker facing the shelf, *We all had our hours reduced because it's the end of the quarter and they have to make their figures for bonuses.* I'm an elderly couple and a mother with toddler away from the pharmacy counter. *Oh yeah, and a raise just went through so they're cutting pa– cutting hours for everyone because of that.*

We'll all be working at a twenty percent cut to labor, so as long as you can do sixty hours of work in twenty hours a week, we'll be fine, he jokes. The worker facing also jokes, says, *I should just move downstairs,* which means the parking garage, *in a cardboard box,* and the one who's off the clock says, *Yeah!* Facing worker then says, *Maybe that's where I'm headed anyway. Thanks for depressing me while I'm still working.*

Now it's my turn, but the worker at the register says my drugs aren't ready. I want to insist, *But I was told they'd be ready at two,* like I think it's important, but instead I stand there, like an asshole. Exhausted and apologetic, she says, *The other pharmacist didn't show up today.*

Michael and I both used to work in grocery stores, and we talk about how it doesn't matter if self-checkout truly *replaces* workers or not, because people, us included, keep standing in human lines even though there are only a couple left, and they keep getting longer, and companies won't stop closing stores and blaming retail theft while cutting jobs and giving the money to bosses as bonuses for doing less than nothing—for doing negative work. If you work in a grocery store, you'll learn about shrink and margins, and you'll never regret stealing again, especially when you work there and still can't afford your groceries.

So the drugs aren't ready, and the person working the register can't tell if there are enough drugs to fill my prescriptions until the lone pharmacist running back and forth between piles of bags of bottles of pills in the back can get to it, and she feels really bad, I can tell, but I think, *Not as bad as me after going without drugs for this long,* softening and bubbling and fading. In the last hour, the line behind me has become longer. She, the person working the register, has the same permanent soft-knit eyebrow stress I wear. I make little enough money that my drugs are free, but not so little that I can't afford to go home and to return. I say, *No big deal. We'll come back tomorrow.* What's another day when this one's almost over? We go to the fucking self-checkout.

I turn up shitty beep boop radio music to lighten the car's atmosphere, and we pull out of the parking lot. We're two blocks removed from Safeway when my phone lights up. *Alert: your prescription is now ready.* But we're already going in a direction, already accepted reality. What are we supposed to do, turn around?

Unwell Beings

Another wasted weekend leaned over the toilet, acid and bile sputtering out, unable to keep even water down until way past dark. My husband says we had a great time the night before, and I'm sure he's right, but now I'm thrown off my medication cycle and will forget to take them on time, which will make me forget to eat and sleep, which will spill over into subsequent days, causing bigger disruptions in the cycle, which may as well be a part of the greater cycle at this point. Rhythmic bumps, reminders to start again. He wishes I were better at managing my health, at handling my liquor. Actually, I don't know if he does, but I also don't know if I do.

It sounds worse than it is when I describe it, the drinking, I'm sure, and I wonder what is normal. I'm a dirtbag most days. I often forget to brush my teeth or wash my face until like 1pm if I do it at all. I don't know if I have anything to say anymore, or if there's a reason to say anything. I'm unsure if it's possible to do or to know anything in a way that matters, or if even that matters.

Krissy sends me a video of two cats in the place she's housesitting and a text-as-caption that reads, "Unwell beings." We became friends by writing for the same satirical music publication, so I hear whispers of a joke set-up and read wry observation in even our normal and serious exchanges. The cats are crammed side by side in the window, backs to her, striking the wall with their tails.

I've been trying to help Krissy, an expert dog person, understand cats. One is twitching the end of its tail, which I tell Krissy means it's intrigued. The other cat is annoyed, its entire tail thumping against the wall.

That's how I feel watching my body's thinnest innermost contents fight their way up my esophagus, yellow and alien-tasting, to drop pathetic in our filthy toilet. I twitch, unsteadied by curiosity, thump my elbows on the lip of the bowl and hold back a sweaty fistful of hair, annoyed by the perfect circle of brown dried blood from some past period against porcelain, only visible from this familiar hunched angle. I should clean more. Mold and dust seem like worse problems on this end of the coast than they were down south. I am looking for something without moving toward it.

I told my two friends named Mark, also from the satirical music publication, that I'd work on a summer playlist over the weekend to swap with them. They made theirs already. Instead, I spend the days working on a music video and drinking, punch the first few cans open in the morning while we mix corn syrup and food coloring into fake blood, and I keep insisting we add cocoa powder, corn starch, old things I pull from the dark backs of cabinets. I pretend to be dead and pretend to kill; I hide in Aaron's bedroom and bag his head in black plastic, paint my friends' faces and bodies cold sticky red, laugh loud and sit in unusual chairs to make room for rare company, and have no memory of the night ending.

Later, when I'm between vomits, Michael asks, "Do you remember me telling you to slow down?" I don't, and I wonder if we are both lying.

He has a point when he says it's impossible to make me happy, sometimes. Or maybe he means that it's impossible for me to feel happy. This is the kind of thing I am always asking him to define and specify for me, especially if we are arguing, which we do often in good and exciting ways, but which we also do badly, particularly when we drink, and the asking feels like an automatic thing, a setting whose lock has been activated, an uncontrollable cycle. "I can tell you've been drinking because we're talking in circles" is a common refrain of mine, whether or not I have also been drinking.

Dreams are uncommon when I take my medications on time, and sometimes I choose alcohol over meds because together they're a bad mix and because the alcohol got there first that day. I dreamed last night that I was loading an old sewing machine, winding red thread around the bobbin and urging the whining of the motor through my foot, the cause of the spinning of the small plastic wheel.

It might not be true, what I said earlier, about being a dirtbag most days and about how eternally I am unraveling shit with Michael. It might be that those days stand out more than all the ones when we are both up in the morning, when he makes eggs or I make oatmeal, when I go to work feeling good and come home feeling good, when we pass a guitar or a book back and forth and I tell him, "I would like to marry you again and again."

"I can't fucking do this again, I don't want to," I insist to his back, meaning "drink alcohol," but really I don't mean it, I mean "be this sick again," because what I believe should be a normal mild hangover keeps snowballing into a day or several without eating or meds, adding beads to a string of sick and useless moments. I'm telling it to him like it's his fault, but really I want a witness, and hate knowing I don't mean it, that I'll dry out for the week, and we'll be right back here.

It's tempting to believe that the misstep is trying to keep up with a career drinker who is older than me, but then I remember how far back my string stretches, the uncountable beads from nights blacked out and driving between cities, showing up to work still drunk, compromising my body for the better part of a decade, and I wonder if I've ever been able to hold liquor, or if it's something that has always poured straight through me.

Words have meaning, but I don't know what "alcoholic" or "addicted" means. It means my mother, who said, "Today is my sobriety chip day," each and every year on my birthday, and never seeing her take a sip, which provided no explanation or warning for the terror of her explosive rage and the completeness of her cold silences.

With Michael, or with Michael and me, I guess it means a kind of predictability, maybe even reliability. It means he will bring me home one of the drinks I like as a treat in a few days after I say I can't do that again. He dries out sometimes for a month or so and forgives himself the occasional drink, so I do, too. For him, but not for myself. I resent the treat drink, but accept it anyway, and other times, I ask him to bring me one.

When Michael and I had our first fling, he told me in the low privacy of my bedroom floor, "People pay attention to you when you speak. You should really check in with that." It felt flattering and warm, but at the same time like being handed a responsibility.

And now I seem to recall that responsibility when I've gone too far, too vivid, in my exorcisms. I say things like, "I don't like you when you drink," like I'm throwing a rock into a nest of ants, and, "Then again I am drinking when I don't like you when you drink, so maybe it's more like, when I drink I don't like who you are when you drink," like I'm sweeping the ants back in.

You have to say things out loud, or at least write them, or at least I do. I think everyone knows Vonnegut said that. "If this isn't nice, I don't know what is."

As I bemoan the time lost to making myself drink until I'm sick, the parts of the music video shoot I don't remember and the ill uselessness that follows, I forget that the video is for fun (no one expects anyone will see it), and for a band I am in, and that I'm finally playing music again, and alongside a person who sees me, sometimes all the way through, with vision like a burning x-ray, in a cold city as far from home as I've ever lived, and it is as if I am living a dream some forgotten, much younger me dreamed.

Or perhaps this is the magical thinking Allison told me is linked with types of anxiety and obsession disorders. No one can convince me that I wouldn't be able to befriend a pack of wolves in the wild, for example. But then again, I also have fantasized about being eaten by wolves, a death I feel would make me more useful to something else than perhaps I have ever been in life. So either way is fine.

Allison is also a comedy writer from the satirical music publication, and it occurs to me that at no point did I used to dream of a life with this many comedy writers in it, swapping sobriety advice, favorite records, tales of mental illness, and punching up one another's lines by asking, "What did you mean when you said this?"

Words mean something, which is why Michael said he was an alcoholic right off the bat, and so easily. Maybe it isn't the most important thing about him in the way that my mother made it seem like the most important thing about her, and maybe it's not the most important thing about her, either. Sometimes you have to work backwards when you are untangling knots.

It's like those string games kids do, cat's cradle and all those, how you'd have to undo each step and go back methodically to figure out how to get it right. Patterns and tension build into brief moments that almost look like magic when you catch them at the right angle, like at my best friend Kate's wedding, after I returned to the barn dance floor from getting her husband to smoke me out and she was sad no one was dancing with her, the flood of sunlight that broke through clouds when Michael appeared like a vision dancing wild among us, when the radiation of his exuberance drew in more dancers and I felt the exact same feelings of shock and relief I had wrestled with, had not understood, the first moment we met: "That's my husband."

I am a dramatic, anguished pile on the couch. Downstairs, where it's underground and cool, Michael composes vibrant, meditative music, all crystal glimmers and electric humming that floats through the floor. Then it falls silent, and he comes upstairs.

"Do you want to come write next to me?"

I follow him down, where he asks my input on these long ambient compositions, and I am of use, and my high-pitched spinning slows to a stop. I tell him the music is perfect to write to. I'm doing it now.

Cante Jondo

"I want something from her, but I don't know what it is. I guess that means sex." —Joey Comeau, "Patricia"

The other night one of the women asked the rest of us, "Have you ever had a crush on a character in a book?"

I have not. I know some people have crushes on dead writers, which is the same thing, though; like Joey Comeau writes of a crush on Patricia Highsmith. I met him once, at a bookstore in San Francisco, where he read his "I think this Coke made me gay" story. His eyes were pink and narrow because he'd been pepper-sprayed recently, and the only thing I remember about the reason for the pepper spraying is that everyone pressing into each other and around the bookshelves laughed when he told us. I said words to him, but they had no recognizable shapes—it was a burbling gold-popping candy efflorescence that showered him, and I think we hugged, because my bones felt the slightness of his bones, and our frames were briefly mirror-to-mirror. He wrote in his dedication to me, "Live for today you little shit. The end is near."

This is not a mean thing to say. He's quoting a character in his book. I take parts of it to heart.

My thing is different because Joey Comeau is not dead as of this writing, which means now he is alive forever. Like a character in a book. Who, okay, I have a crush on. And it is also different because I could, in theory, write *to* him, rather than *about*. But I think crushes are more *about* than *to*.

When the woman asked the question, I was in shock. The other women and I had just been standing around a free-form fireworks setup (this being out in the cuts, but I don't know if they call it that there, in Pennsylvania). We crouched underneath the lights as they escaped the orange tubes and exploded and boomed deep in our skulls, our jaws, our throats, colossal expansion in our chests, and their ash rained and twirled down on us like it was beaten out of a burning piñata, graying our hair.

All of us women, we'd screamed as a chorus, voices stretched by helplessness into those of little girls. Something so much bigger than us suddenly seizing our bodies, from the inside out, and the tangle of their soft arms as they fell together while I fell apart and away and smoldered about it.

So I was hearing, but not listening. This is the exhilaration of battle? That we attempt to replicate? Bodies rattled and pounding long after its echo has faded?

Tía Antonieta sent me a copy of *Poema Del Cante Jondo* for Christmas when I was thirteen and starting to feel certain that everything about the way our country's government and economy functioned was antithetical to human life. Maybe it was thirteen-year-old morbidity or just a personal inclination toward tragedy, but after I was moved by Federico García Lorca's words—I read them in Spanish and English side by side—I fell in sick sorrowful romance with his death. There he was, dead and gone, on *London Calling,* which Papi, who was staying with his sister that year, away from us, sent me, also for Christmas, because he'd loved it when he was young. This was how I learned about the Spanish Civil War. I didn't learn that I had been shaped by its ripples through blood until way later.

Then Papi took me to Spain. It is the only time I have left North America. It was the War on Terror years, and everyone hated Americans, Papi and me included. We liked punk rock and thought we were smarter than everyone and the son jarocho music of his voice made us both seem like Mexicans in Spain. Foreigners no matter what, no matter where. In Granada, I drank beer and wine and espresso. I looked and looked and looked, and my eyes drank but did not swallow, and are still holding it.

Lorca's childhood home had become a museum, and we arrived as it was closing. No more tours for the day. A man also named Federico, who usually worked the desk, took pity on us and the two German women who'd also come late to the murdered poet's museum, so after the last tour wrapped up and the official guide left, Federico brought us inside.

He was like a Lorca superfan, pointing out the first name thing, excitement vibrating off him, white-gray hair all shocked out as if by lightning strike. When we got to the piano, the ringing of whose hammered strings, according to Federico, was the joyous signal to everyone who could hear that Lorca was home, Federico looked at us like he was waiting for something nice to happen.

"No one is supposed to touch the piano during a tour," he said, Papi translating. "But I have always wanted to hear it, and I don't play myself, and the museum is closed, so this isn't a tour."

A little bubble rose in my belly. I looked to the German women, who shook their heads no. I looked at Papi, who smiled at me in a way I shied from, like the sun. More bubbles rose and burst, faded. Then his expression changed, like, *I can't believe you're about to fucking pass this up,* like the string of half-heated half-playful curses usually reserved for the dog who I think he loved more than anyone, pinche perra pendeja.

I felt sick. Never practiced enough. But I wanted to hear it, too, the sound of Lorca coming back home. I wanted to touch it, like touching Lorca's fingers with mine.

This might be lazy of me, or unskilled, but I am dogshit at describing the sounds that comprise music. I sat down and the wooden chair creaked, bright and chirpy. I stumbled through some bars of "Moonlight Sonata." I like sad music, no surprise.

The noise of Lorca's strings wavered with and within me. Though I might not be able to tell you how his piano sounded when my fingers stroked and urged its smooth keys to crying, when I pressed down on its pedal, first gentle, slow, long, then sudden and hard, so that it whimpered and whined, ay! I can hear it, because my ears took it in their mouths, and did not swallow its deep song.

I know Federico García Lorca is gay, and dead, but his face from a postcard I've kept on every wall since high school was the only image that flickered to the surface when I thought about my answer to the question of crushing on book characters. I didn't say it, though.

It was that he had played with so many forms: music, theater, dance, words, communicating with the speed of life. It was that he had been executed by cowards who waste life in futile pursuit of control. It was that they took him at night, that they'd shot him in the ass twice for being queer, that they still don't know where his body is, resting place bare and unmarked, perhaps feeding an olive grove. It was that his lover was said to have died a year to the day of his death in one of the trenches ("full of poets," in the Clash song).

So, the question, again. My chest was a cavern, still, gaping open after the fireworks' sound receded from it. I was compelled to run into traffic or kick over a trash can. I was compelled to kiss someone, shatter whole relationships and families with just the detonation of my mouth, to walk unseen in the dark past sleeping campers and hiss.

I was compelled to say Lorca, to say Joey Comeau, to say You.

Acknowledgements

To Emily Costa, Aaron Burch, Felicia Urso and D.T. Robbins, Ryan-Ashley Anderson Maloney and Kevin Maloney, Becca Schuh and Monika Ostrowska, Alan Good, August Edwards, and every editor and reader who worked with these essays, thank you forever.

Michael Wheaton, thank you for guiding me through every step of this book with enthusiasm and understanding, for helping me ask the right questions, for being in it with me. Thank you Amy Wheaton for a cover so perfect I didn't even have to ask for it.

Krissy Howard, Allison Mick, Dom Turek, Mark Bouchard, Mark Hassenfratz, Liam Senior, Brett McCabe, John Danek, Zac Von Lux, Dan Rice: I've never felt more of use (happy) than when we wrote jokes together. Ian Kappos, Karter Mycroft, Barton Aikman, Joshua Duke: if I could make another Los Suelos with you I would, especially if we got someone else to pay for it again. Olga Murillo, Blanca Muñoz, Sharlene Huynh, Will Godbey, Andrew Liu, J.J. Prado, Rosie Ruiz: I've never felt more out of my mind (alive) than when we wrote stories and poems and studied together. Jillian Luft, Kirsti MacKenzie, Kristen Felicetti, Shelby Hinte, Rax Will, Rick Paulas, Tucker Leighty-Phillips, Joshua Turek, Barrelhouse Writer Camp '24 and the continued contingent at AWP '25, and everyone who's shared time, work, readings, and whatever else it is that suggests a literary kinship: I'm so stoked that I found you.

Carmella Ortiz, Jennifer Andrew, Kate Estrada, Matt Nielsen, Cliff Mattis, Sam Sipin, Bee Spiderman, Jason Heiser, Willa Leach, Bob Price, the Knight family, Aaron Kasson, Samantha Kasch, Heather Heywood, Ben Heywood, Anthony Razo, Kenny Becker, Chris Watson, Mary Kobayashi, Molly Bauer, and the too many others to name who kept me alive and inspired, played music or made something with me, shared a meal, let me crash, and otherwise stuck around: Thank you.

Thanks to Doug Rice, Josh McKinney, Helen Lee, Stephen Cooper, Michael Wyly, Jack Schouten, and every teacher who saw what I was trying to do.

To Papi, my mom, Gaby, Chayo, Vivi, los twinquis, Gramma, Heather, Javi, and Chris: my love for you is too big for words. Michael Sparks Jr., thank you for being there, in sun and shadow. And Dylan: I love you more every year since you left.

These essays, or early versions of them, first appeared in: *Neutral Spaces, Jarnal Vol.1* (Mason Jar Press), *Triangle House Review* Issue 29, *Fourteen Hills* No.29, *Sundog* Issue 18*, Hobart, Death of Print, Rejection Letters, Farewell Transmission* Issue 1, and *Pool Party.*

About the Author

Lauren Lavín was made in Mexico, born in Oakland, and currently lives in Seattle.

— also from Autofocus Books —

Duplex — Mike Nagel

XO — Sara Rauch

Until It Feels Right — Emily Costa

Cleave — Holly Pelesky

Nextdoor in Colonialtown — Ryan Rivas

Too Much Tongue — Adrienne Marie Barrios & Leigh Chadwick

Picture Window — Danny Caine

the nature machine! — Tyler Gillespie

A Kind of In-Between — Aaron Burch

How to Write a Novel: An Anthology of 20 Craft Essays About Writing, None of Which Ever Mention Writing — ed. Aaron Burch

Hiraeth — Mistie R. Watkins

That Spell — Tate N. Oquendo

My Modest Blindness — Russell Brakefield

A Calendar Is A Snakeskin — Kristine Langley Mahler

Culdesac — Mike Nagel

Razed by TV Sets — Jason McCall

In the Away Time — Kristen E. Nelson

The Body Is A Temporary Gathering Place — Andrew Bertaina

Daughterhood — Emily Adrian

A Healthy Interest in the Lives of Others — Teresa Carmody

Yes I Am Human I Know You Were Wondering — Erin Dorney

Leave: A Postpartum Account — Shayne Terry

Out There In the Dark — Katharine Coldiron

If I Can Be Honest: Selected Prose from the Four Years of Autofocus Lit (2020-2024) — ed. Michael Wheaton

The Dead Dad Diaries — Erin Slaughter

A Revionist History of Loving Men — Lena Ziegler

Marginalia — Naomi Washer

Tacoma — Aaron Burch

Teen Queen Training: Essays after The Seventeen Book of Etiquette and Entertaining, 1963 — Kristine Langley Mahler